MAY 2017

SandCastle

Compound Words

rattle + snake = rattlesnake

Amanda Rondeau

Consulting Editor Monica Marx, M.A./Reading Specialist

ABDO
Publishing Company

Published by SandCastle™, an imprint of ABDO Publishing Company, 4940 Viking Drive, Edina, Minnesota 55435.

Printed in the United States.

Credits
Edited by: Pam Price
Curriculum Coordinator: Nancy Tuminelly
Cover and Interior Design and Production: Mighty Media
Photo Credits: Comstock, Digital Vision, Eyewire Images, Hemera, PhotoDisc, Rubberball Productions, ThinkStock

Library of Congress Cataloging-in-Publication Data

Rondeau, Amanda, 1974-
    Rattle + snake = rattlesnake / Amanda Rondeau.
        p. cm. -- (Compound words)
    Includes index.
    Summary: Illustrations and easy-to-read text introduce compound words related to hiking and camping.
    ISBN 1-59197-437-2
    1. English language--Compound words--Juvenile literature. [1. English language--Compound words.] I. Title: Rattle plus snake equals rattlesnake. II. Title.

PE1175.R6676 2003
428.1--dc21

2003048121

SandCastle™ books are created by a professional team of educators, reading specialists, and content developers around five essential components that include phonemic awareness, phonics, vocabulary, text comprehension, and fluency. All books are written, reviewed, and leveled for guided reading, early intervention reading, and Accelerated Reader® programs and designed for use in shared, guided, and independent reading and writing activities to support a balanced approach to literacy instruction.

Let Us Know

After reading the book, SandCastle would like you to tell us your stories about reading. What is your favorite page? Was there something hard that you needed help with? Share the ups and downs of learning to read. We want to hear from you! To get posted on the ABDO Publishing Company Web site, send us e-mail at:

sandcastle@abdopub.com

SandCastle Level: Transitional

A compound word is two words joined together to make a new word.

rattle + snake =

rattlesnake

A rattlesnake is dangerous.

Its fangs inject poison.

earth + worm =

earthworm

Eva does not want
to touch the
earthworm.

It is slimy.

watch + dog =

watchdog

Beth thinks Spot is the best watchdog.

fire + wood =

firewood

Evan helps his
grandpa stack
firewood.

up + hill =

uphill

Ray and Joe climb uphill on their hike.

camp + fire =

campfire

The Hall family sits by a campfire on their desert vacation.

Earthworms and Rattlesnakes

Joe packed his backpack for camp.

Then he hiked uphill,
where it was not so damp.

Joe took Buster, his watchdog,
to save him from rattlesnakes.

But Buster was not so brave;
he only wanted the pancakes!

In the middle of the night, Buster started to bark.

Did you know that earthworms and rattlesnakes look the same in the dark?

21

More Compound Words

anthill	meadowlark
campground	moonlight
diamondback	nightfall
evergreen	nighttime
firefly	outdoors
flashlight	outhouse
groundhog	outside
hummingbird	wildcat
ladybug	woodpecker

Glossary

dangerous   not safe

desert   an area that is dry and sandy and has few plants because there is very little rain

earthworm   a worm that digs through the ground and eats dirt

firewood   wood that is burned in fires

rattlesnake   a snake that lives in North and South America and has a segmented tail that makes a rattling noise when shaken

23

About SandCastle™

A professional team of educators, reading specialists, and content developers created the SandCastle™ series to support young readers as they develop reading skills and strategies and increase their general knowledge. The SandCastle™ series has four levels that correspond to early literacy development in young children. The levels are provided to help teachers and parents select the appropriate books for young readers.

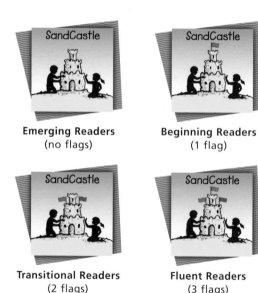

Emerging Readers
(no flags)

Beginning Readers
(1 flag)

Transitional Readers
(2 flags)

Fluent Readers
(3 flags)

These levels are meant only as a guide. All levels are subject to change.

To see a complete list of SandCastle™ books and other nonfiction titles from ABDO Publishing Company, visit www.abdopub.com or contact us at:

4940 Viking Drive, Edina, Minnesota 55435 • 1-800-800-1312 • fax: 1-952-831-1632